50 THINGS YOU DIDN'T KNOW ABOUT MEXICO

**Written and Illustrated
by Sean O'Neill**

RED
CHAIR
•PRESS•

Egremont, Massachusetts

50 Things You Didn't Know About is produced and published by Red Chair Press:
www.redchairpress.com

FREE lesson guide at www.redchairpress.com/free-activities

Publisher's Cataloging-In-Publication Data

(Provided by Cassidy Cataloging Services, Inc)

Names: O'Neill, Sean, 1968- author, illustrator. | O'Neill, Sean, 1968
  50 things you didn't know about (Series)

Title: 50 things you didn't know about Mexico / written and illustrated by
  Sean O'Neill.

Other Titles: Mexico

Description: Egremont, Massachusetts : Red Chair Press, [2024] | Interest
  age level: 006-009. | Includes bibliographical references and index. |
  Summary: With 50 Things You Didn't Know About Mexico, young readers
  will learn about Mexico's history and ancient cultures, discover unique
  foods and learn about daily life in this fascinating country.--Publisher.

Identifiers: ISBN: 978-1-64371-324-3 (library hardcover) | 978-1-64371-325-0
  (softcover) | 978-164371-326-7 (ebook) | LCCN: 2023936992

Subjects: LCSH: Mexico--History--Juvenile literature. | Mexico--Description
  and travel--Juvenile literature. | Mexico--Social life and customs--
  Juvenile literature. | CYAC: Mexico--History. | Mexico--Description
  and travel. | Mexico--Social life and customs. | BISAC: JUVENILE
  NONFICTION / Travel. | JUVENILE NONFICTION / People & Places /
  Mexico.

Classification: LCC: F1208.5 .O54 2024 | DDC: 972--dc23

Printed in the United States of America

0524 1P F24CG

TABLE of CONTENTS

NATURAL WONDERS

With 7,000 miles of coastline, Mexico is famous worldwide for the tropical beauty of its beaches. But Mexico's rich **biodiversity** offers more than just sun, sand, and surf. High desert in the north, fertile plateaus in the central valleys, as well as rainforest, mountains, canyons, and even a few volcanoes combine to create habitats for a wide variety of plant and animal life, making Mexico truly a land of natural wonders.

1 Mexico is one of the most biologically diverse countries in the world. It is home to 26,000 species of plants, 1,200 kinds of reptiles, over one thousand species of birds and about 500 species of mammals, including, of course, the jaguar.

2 One of the most amazing species of reptile in Mexico is the collared lizard. Named for the two black stripes around its neck, this quick little lizard uses its tail for balance and can run on two legs like an Olympic sprinter.

3 The huge asteroid that is believed to have caused the **extinction** of the dinosaurs 65 million years ago struck the Earth in Mexico–specifically near the current town of Chicxulub on Mexico's Yucatán peninsula.

THAT CAN'T BE GOOD...

BOOM

4 The Mesoamerican Reef off the coast of Yucatán is the world's second-largest coral reef and is home to hundreds of species of sea life, including fish, turtles and sharks.

5 Every year in November, millions of monarch butterflies make the 2,500 mile journey from the United States and Canada south to central Mexico. The butterflies gather in the Mexican state of Michoacán, where the Mexican government has created a national refuge for them.

6 Butterflies and tourists aren't the only ones that like to spend the winter in Mexico. Each December thousands of gray whales swim from Alaska to give birth in the warm water off the coast of Mexico.

7 One of the most impressive creatures native to Mexico is the quetzal bird. Its long, green tail feathers were used to decorate the headdresses of ancient Aztec rulers, and in ancient times, killing a quetzal was punishable by death.

NOW THAT'S WHAT I CALL RED!

8 When Spanish explorers arrived in Mexico in the 16th century, they learned of a native insect called *cochineal* that could be used to make bright red paints and dyes. Because Europeans loved red for royal garments, this little bug became one of the most valuable exports from the New World.

ANCIENT CIVILIZATIONS

Throughout history, Mexico's rich natural landscape has given rise to many great civilizations. At different periods in history, **indigenous** cultures such as the *Olmec*, *Maya*, *Toltec*, and *Aztec* ruled parts of Mexico. As archaeologists continue to unearth remnants of these historic civilizations, we're learning more and more about how truly amazing they were.

9 The oldest known civilization to have lived in Mexico is the *Olmec*. Very little is known about this ancient culture, but they left behind mysterious stone sculptures of giant heads–some as large as 11 feet tall and weighing 30 tons.

10 Ancient Maya farmers were masters of an agricultural system called irrigation, in which water is diverted to dry areas in order to water crops.

11 One of the most important crops grown by Maya and Aztec farmers was the *cacao* bean, better known to us as chocolate (from the Aztec word *xocolatl*.) Cacao beans were dried, ground up, and mixed with honey and hot water–the world's first hot chocolate!

12 Chocolate wasn't just for drinking. It was such a desirable crop that the ancient Aztecs also used cacao beans as currency, or money. 100 beans could buy you a turkey, and 60,000 to buy a jade necklace.

13 Hot chocolate might sound pretty good, but you might be less interested in other parts of the ancient Mexican diet. Maya and Aztecs enjoyed crunchy grasshoppers and caterpillars called maguey worms.

14 The Maya and the Aztecs both were experts at building pyramids. The famous temple of Kukulkan in the Maya city of Chichen Itza has exactly 365 steps to the top– one for each day of the year.

15 The largest pyramid in Mexico is the Temple of Cholula, although, until fairly recently, nobody even knew it was there! It had been so overgrown with plants and vegetation, people assumed it was just a big hill until archaeologists began excavating it in the 1930s.

16 The Aztecs believed in many frightening gods. The war god Huitzilopochtli was armed with a fire serpent, and his evil sister Coyolxauhqui, goddess of the moon, according to legend, murdered her own mother.

17 Ancient Maya were very knowledgeable about the movements of the stars and planets. They observed the planet Venus closely, and when they saw it in the sky, it was a sign to go to war. They called this a "star war."

MAY THE FORCE BE WITH YOU.

18 Rubber trees grow throughout Mexico, and the Maya learned how to tap the sap from these trees and use it to make waterproof cloth, glue, and even rubber balls.

19 Another type of sap from a tree called the sapodilla was called *chicle* and turned rubbery when chewed. That's right– the Maya invented chewing gum! In fact, *chicle* from the Yucatán was used to make gum up until the 1940s.

20 The primary grain product in ancient Mexico was corn, or *maize*. The Aztecs and Maya used this to make everything from tortillas to popcorn.

21 Both the Maya and the Aztecs played a ball game called *tlachtli*. Teams of two or three players wearing headdresses and large belts would try to hit a rubber ball through a stone ring. Much like Roman gladiators, the losers were usually put to death.

22 Pyramids weren't the only thing the Maya had in common with ancient Egypt. Like hieroglyphics, the Maya had an ancient writing system based on pictograms, or glyphs, and wrote on paper made from tree bark.

23 Among many other important contributions, the Aztecs may have invented something very important to this book: cartoon speech bubbles! In Aztec pictograms, small blue bubbles above a figure's head indicated when they were speaking.

24 Both the Aztecs and Maya made detailed calendars. According to Aztec legend, the world would end and a new one would begin every 52 years. This occasion was marked by a New Fire Ceremony, where the entire city was darkened, and new fire was brought to every home in the city.

YOUR NEW FIRE, MA'AM.

25 The arrival of Spanish invaders in the early 16th century led to the downfall of indigenous cultures in Mexico. The Spanish conquest of Mexico was brutal, but their most effective weapons were diseases like smallpox which killed huge numbers of Aztecs and Maya.

26 The glory of ancient civilizations may be in the past, but these great cultures are still with us. Today there are still about 6 million Mexican citizens with Mayan heritage. About 2 million more live in Central America.

A NEW NATION

Following the discovery by Europeans of the American continents in the late 15th century, the Spanish began conquering the native peoples and setting up a colonial outpost that they called New Spain. After the arrival of the Spanish, life would never be the same, but years of conflict and struggle against Spanish occupation would eventually lead to the birth of a new nation: Mexico.

27 The colony of New Spain included all of what is now Mexico, as well as parts of Florida, Texas, California, New Mexico, Arizona and Nevada. These lands became part of the U.S. as a result of the Mexican-American War of 1846.

28 When the Spanish arrived and created New Spain, they established their capital on the site of the Tenochtitlán. It stands today as the modern capital, Mexico City.

29 The Mexican flag features an unusual image: a golden eagle on a cactus eating a snake. According to Aztec legend, wandering Aztecs were told by their god to find an eagle on a cactus eating a snake. When they found one, that's where they built their capital, Tenochtitlán.

30 The Spanish colonists created the world's first international currency, or money. In Mexico, they minted silver coins which were used throughout the Caribbean, Europe, and even Asia. These coins were called "pieces of eight," because each one was worth eight *reals* in Spain.

31 Mexico is home to the oldest university in North America. The National Autonomous University of Mexico was founded in 1551, 85 years before Harvard in Massachusetts.

32 A controversial figure in Mexican history is a Maya woman named Malintzin (*la Malinche* in Spanish). Because she spoke Nahuatl, the language of the Aztecs, the Spanish forced her to act as a translator during their invasion. She is honored for her survival skills by some, but seen as a traitor by others.

33 After 200 years of Spanish rule, many Mexicans were ready to govern themselves. The Mexican independence movement began on September 16, 1810, when a Mexican priest named Father Hidalgo y Costilla rang a bell and shouted, "*¡Viva la Mexico!*" (long live Mexico) from the church tower. Sept. 16 is Mexico's Independence Day.

19

34 One of the heroes of the independence movement was General Antonio de Santa Anna. Santa Anna lost his leg to cannon fire during a battle in Veracruz. Later, he had the leg transported to Mexico City and gave it a full military burial with honors.

35 The road to independence was a long and bumpy one. In 1863, the French invaded Mexico and installed Austrian Archduke Ferdinand Maximilian as emperor. Yes, Mexico had an emperor! It didn't last long, though. Maximilian was overthrown and executed a few years later.

36 Although his reign was short, Maximilian did take the time to build a castle, which makes his home, Chapultepec Castle, the only royal castle in North America.

I'M NOT SURE ABOUT THE HAT...

37 One of the most admired leaders in Mexican history is President Benito Juarez. He took over after the fall of Archduke Ferdinand. He rebuilt the Mexican economy and improved the lives of ordinary people. He is sometimes called "the Abraham Lincoln of Mexico."

38 Revolution came to Mexico again in the early 1900s, when revolutionaries Pancho Villa and Emiliano Zapata led uprisings against corruption in the Mexican government. Both men are remembered as heroes for standing up for the poor.

21

CHAPTER 4

TRADITIONS AND CULTURE

The Mexican people are a diverse group. There are many people with indigenous, or native, heritage, some of European and Asian background, many descendants of Africans brought centuries ago as slaves, and, by far the largest group, are people called *mestizos*, or mixed, whose background is a mixture of Spanish and Native ancestry. But, together, all of these people share a rich and vibrant culture that is distinctly Mexican.

MMMMM

39 One of the most popular celebrations in Mexico is *Dia de los Muertos*, or Day of the Dead. Although it is held at the beginning of November, and features skulls and skeletons, it has no relationship to Halloween. The origins of the holiday go back to Aztec rituals and celebrations around death.

40 Despite its focus on death, Dia de los Muertos is a lively celebration. There are street parades, women dress as *La Calavera Catrina* (the Elegant Skull) and children eat sugar skulls and *pan de muerto* (bread of the dead).

23

41 A familiar sight at many Mexican celebrations is a piñata. This fun tradition goes back to the ancient Maya, who hit ceramic pots covered in feathers to release treats stored inside.

42 One of the most famous Mexicans in history is the artist Frida Kahlo. She is known for her colorful self-portraits that celebrate indigenous Mexican culture, and also tell the story of her lifelong suffering due to a childhood traffic accident.

43 Many of Kahlo's self-portraits show her with animals native to Mexico. This wasn't just artistic license. She kept many exotic animals as pets, including spider monkeys, a fawn, an Amazon parrot, an eagle, macaws, parakeets, hens, sparrows, and a rare breed of hairless dog called a Mexican *ixquintle*.

44 Mexican citizens in other fields have reached the greatest heights—literally! In 1985, Rodolfo Neri Vela became the first Mexican astronaut. Six years later, American Ellen Ochoa was the first woman of Mexican **heritage** in space.

CHAPTER 5

DAILY LIFE

When most people think of Mexico, what often comes to mind are beautiful beaches with gentle breezes and palm trees. This may be the experience of the millions of tourists that visit the country, but for the locals, life is a little different. Most Mexicans today live in large, bustling, modern cities such as Mexico City, the world's fifth largest city, with over 21 million people.

45 With 124 million Spanish speakers, Mexico has by far the largest Spanish-speaking population in the world.

46 Mexico is a very popular destination for travelers. More than 30 million tourists visit the country each year to explore the beautiful beaches and historical archaeological sites throughout the country.

47 Color TV was invented in Mexico. Mexican inventor Guillermo González Camarena created the chromoscopic adapter for television equipment, which was an early color TV transmission system. His first official color transmission was from Mexico City in 1946.

48 A popular pastime for many Mexicans is boating through a network of canals in an area called Xochimilco. It's not just a fun way to spend a Sunday afternoon. These waterways are the last remnants of a vast system of canals built by the Aztecs centuries ago.

49 Many tourists know of Yucatán: legend has it that the region's name came from a misunderstanding. A Spanish explorer supposedly asked a local Maya the name of the area. The Maya replied, "*Ma'anaatik ka t'ann,*" which means "I don't understand you." And the name stuck.

WHAT DO YOU CALL THIS LAND?

50 We all know that cowboys roamed the open ranges of the American West, but there were many Mexican cowboys as well. These *vaqueros*, as they were called, are part of a proud tradition of horse-riding and cattle raising going back to **medieval** Spain.

Glossary

biodiversity: he rich and widely different types of animal and plant life of a place

extinction: when something goes out of existence or disappears

heritage: something related to someone's family history

indigenous: being from a place since recorded history began

medieval: from the Middle Ages, about 500 to 1500

Explore More

Cipriano, Jeri. *Mexico, Hello Neighbor series.* Red Chair Press, 2019.

Deal-Márguez, Isela and Xitali Gómez. *Your Passport to Mexico.* Capstone Press, 2022.

Katz, Susan B. *The Story of Frida Kahlo.* Rockridge Press, 2020.

Walters, Jennifer Marino. *Ellen Ochoa: Breaking Barriers in Space.* Red Chair Press, 2024.

Index

About the Author/Illustrator

Sean O'Neill is an illustrator and writer living in Chicago. He is the creator of *50 Things You Didn't Know* and the *Rocket Robinson* series of graphic novels. Sean loves history, trivia, and drawing cartoons, so this project is pretty much a dream assignment. He's sorry he wasn't in Mexico City while writing the book.